BMX
FREESTYLE

BY RAY McCLELLAN

BELLWETHER MEDIA • MINNEAPOLIS, MN

Are you ready to take it to the extreme?
Torque books thrust you into the action-packed world
of sports, vehicles, and adventure. These books may
include dirt, smoke, fire, and dangerous stunts.
WARNING: Read at your own risk.

This edition first published in 2008 by Bellwether Media.

No part of this publication may be reproduced in whole or in part without written
permission of the publisher. For information regarding permission, write to Bellwether
Media Inc., Attention: Permissions Department, 5357 Penn Avenue South, Minneapolis,
MN 55419.

Library of Congress Cataloging-in-Publication Data

McClellan, Ray.
 BMX freestyle / by Ray McClellan.
    p. cm. -- (Torque : action sports)
 Summary: "Amazing photography accompanies engaging information about BMX
freestyle. The combination of high-interest subject matter and light text is intended for
students in grades 3 through 7"--Provided by publisher.
 Includes bibliographical references and index.
 ISBN-13: 978-1-60014-138-6 (hardcover : alk. paper)
 ISBN-10: 1-60014-138-2 (hardcover : alk. paper)
 1. Bicycle motocross--Juvenile literature. 2. Stunt cycling--Juvenile literature. I. Title.

 GV1049.3.M42 2008
 796.6'2--dc22

                                                        2007042404

CONTENTS

EXIT

WHAT IS BMX FREESTYLE?

Skilled BMX freestyle riders can balance their bodies and move their bikes in ways that seem almost unbelievable. BMX freestyle is also called bicycle stunt riding. It's **acrobatics** on wheels.

BMX freestyle grew out of **BMX racing** in the 1970s. BMX stands for bicycle motocross. It is the sport of racing bicycles on dirt tracks with many jumps and turns. BMX racers had free time between races. They started inventing tricks. BMX freestyle quickly became a sport of its own.

BMX freestyle includes several different forms. In **flatland freestyle**, riders do tricks on flat pavement. **Street freestyle** involves using ledges, rails, and other natural street features for tricks. **Vert freestyle** tricks are performed in vert ramps or empty swimming pools.

Vert ramps are half-pipes, usually at least 8 feet (2.4 meters) tall, with steep sides that become vertical at the top. No matter what form it takes, BMX freestyle is not about speed. It's about courage, creativity, and skill.

Fast Fact

Haro is the company that made the first BMX bikes specifically for stunt riding. The first models are now collector's items.

BMX FREESTYLE EQUIPMENT

BMX freestyle bikes are designed for doing stunts. The tires are slick. Slick tires get the best **traction** on flat surfaces. Freestyle bikes also have stunt pegs in the center of the back wheels and sometimes on the front wheels. Riders balance on the pegs for many tricks.

Bike frames often have extra curves or sections where the tube is flattened. Riders may stand on these curves or flattened sections during tricks.

Brakes are an interesting feature on freestyle bikes. Freestylers invented a design that threads brake cables through the bike's tubes. This gets the cables out of the rider's way. It also allows riders to spin their handlebars a full 360 degrees without getting twisted up in cables.

15

Freestylers must pay attention to safety. Falling on hard pavement while doing a stunt can cause injuries. Helmets are essential. Riders also wear long-sleeved shirts and long pants to protect their skin.

BMX FREESTYLE IN ACTION

There are hundreds of tricks in BMX freestyle. Many moves are the same as ones done in freestyle motocross or skateboarding. A **grind** is when the rider slides the pegs down a rail or ledge. A **manual** is popping the front wheel in the air and moving forward on the back wheel without peddling. No-handers are also common. Riders are constantly inventing new tricks that build off the basic ones.

The popularity of BMX freestyle has exploded since 1995. That was the year of the first ESPN Extreme Games in Rhode Island. Every year since then they have been called the X Games. This major competition and others like it have brought BMX freestyle to the attention of millions of people. Freestyle daredevils such as Dave Mirra and Mat Hoffman have become international celebrities.

fast fact

Some freestyle bikes have only one brake. Some have no brakes at all. Only the experts can manage bikes that have no brakes.

GLOSSARY

acrobatics—the sport of doing athletic stunts that involve jumping, balancing, tumbling, and swinging

BMX racing—the sport of racing bicycles around tracks

flatland freestyle—a BMX freestyle form that involves doing tricks on a flat, paved surface

grind—a trick in which the bike moves forward with the pegs balanced on the edge of something

manual—a trick in which the bike moves forward on the rear wheel with the front wheel in the air; the rider does not pedal in this trick.

street freestyle—a BMX freestyle form that involves using ledges, rails, steps, and other street features to do tricks

traction—the grip of the tires on a riding surface

vert freestyle—vert is short for vertical; vert freestyle is doing tricks while riding up and down ramps that become vertical at the top.

TO LEARN MORE

AT THE LIBRARY

David, Jack. *BMX Racing*. Minneapolis, Minn.: Bellwether, 2008.

Doeden, Matt. *BMX Freestyle*. Mankato, Minn.: Capstone, 2006.

Maurer, Tracy. *BMX Freestyle*. Vero Beach, Fla.: Rourke, 2001.

ON THE WEB

Learning more about BMX freestyle is as easy as 1, 2, 3.

1. Go to www.factsurfer.com
2. Enter "BMX freestyle" into search box.
3. Click the "Surf" button and you will see a list of related web sites.

With factsurfer.com, finding more information is just a click away.

INDEX